Love Stories:

Writing a Romance Novella in Thirty Days or Less

A Romance In A Month How-To Book

Rachelle Ayala
Lovely Hearts Press
> > > < < <

Contact Rachelle at
http://smarturl.it/ContactRachelle

>>><<<

Dedication
The writers in my Romance In A Month group. Thank
you for sharing your romance writing experiences
with me.

TABLE OF CONTENTS

Preface

Romance Writers, do you want to:

Keep your name in front of your readers with more releases and titles?

Learn why you should write shorter in order to write quicker?

Meet and exceed your yearly writing goals?

Participate in multi-author boxed sets for increased visibility and profit?

Claim your fair share of your reader's attention span among today's tsunami of information by producing a series of novellas or episodic serials?

Make more money while writing less?

If you do, you must master the art of writing shorter works while still providing your readers that great experience of your personal brand of storytelling and character voice.

In today's ebook market, visibility is enhanced by always having something new in front of readers. After a reader closes your book, there are literally millions of offerings competing for her attention: books by other authors, video games, apps, movie clips, social media, chats and forums, and online parties.

The very best time for you to grab a reader and hold her attention is to have another story for her to read right away while she's still basking in the afterglow of the story she just finished.

It's really a no-brainer.

You either have a tremendous backlist like Nora Roberts or Stephen King, or you must build one quickly and effectively.

Writing novellas will do that for you. Trust me.

In today's attention deficit world of instant messages and news bites, you as a writer will need to figure out how to write compelling novellas that will keep readers coming back for more.

You will build your author platform faster, gain more fans, and make more money. Who doesn't want to do that?

In this book, I'm going to show all the ways to leverage your novellas to gain market share and increase your visibility with readers. I will also show you how to consistently write engaging and high quality stories that will entertain and enrich your readers.

What is a Novella?

Short answer: A complete story in twenty to forty thousand words. (Romance Writers of America definition).

Yes, this is arbitrary, and you're welcome to scour the internet on the debate of actual word count, but I'm betting you want to get started and leave the academic research to others.

Since we want to write high quality novellas, we will not focus solely on word count, but explore the characteristics that make a novella the beast that it is.

A novella is a complete story. It has a beginning, a middle, and an ending. It has characters that need to be introduced and developed. It has conflict, change, motivation, and goals. It has concrete settings that have to be described. And most importantly, it has a story arc, a plot where something important is desired, something important is risked, and the final resolution is satisfying and complete.

A novella tells a story and moves on. It presents a complete plotline with character development and change, but it does not pad the story with expositions and description of a complete world. It will not teach you the history of the Viking invasion, nor will it send you to a world where the laws of physics have to be redefined.

We're very familiar with the novella form in theater, music, and film. Scheherazade was a master of the novella form with her One Thousand and One Arabian nights, designed to be almost told in a single night. She wanted to keep her head, so she not only had to tell an interesting story and one that didn't put the king to sleep, but also one timed for a cliffhanger just before dawn. The next evening, she would finish the story from the preceding night, having saved herself from being beheaded, and start another novella length story.

Fairy tales are also novella length. They are understood as complete stories with characters who undergo change through the journey of the story, but do not take side trips. Each story focuses on a single set of characters with clearly defined protagonist, villain, obstacles and resolutions.

A good example of a popular novella is Charles Dicken's, *A Christmas Carol*. It is a complete story where the main character, Ebenezer Scrooge, transforms from a miserly tightwad to a generous benefactor of humanity.

Other famous novellas include *Animal Farm* by George Orwell, *Of Mice and Men* by John Steinbeck, *The Strange Case of Dr. Jekyll and Mr. Hyde* by Robert

Louis Stevenson, and *The House on Mango Street* by Sandra Cisneros.

A novella is not a short story, a slice-of-life, a vignette, a plot outline or a synopsis. It must be a fully fleshed out story with an ending which resolves the important story questions. Cliffhangers are a possibility, but the story must still feel complete except for the cliffhanger.

Novellas are like movies. Succinct and finished in one afternoon or a few hours.

Novellas are like the sonata form in music: three parts, exposition, development, recapitulation, as opposed to a complete symphony with four long movements.

Novellas are packed with action, show versus tell, but beware, a novella is not simple. It can be every bit as messy, personal, complicated, and twisted as a longer novel. The only difference is it does not meander or explore. It always has a direction and every scene has a definite purpose of moving the story forward.

So there you have it. A novella in a nutshell is a complete story consisting of twenty to forty thousand words.

Why Write a Novella?

A novella is a strange creature much like a Dr. Doolittle's pushmi-pullyu. It's either too long, or too short, and for many, many years, publishers didn't know what to do with them.

They were too long to be packaged in short story collections or published in magazines, but too short to produce as a full-fledged book that would justify a price high enough to recuperate the overhead of print and paper.

So, novellas languished, and writers were encouraged to go long with full-length novels, the more epic, the better.

Stephen King said he couldn't publish novellas because "they were too long to be short and too short to be really long." That was before the ebook revolution where publishers eyed the bottom line in terms of how much they could charge per page.

Enter the twenty-first century filled with e-readers and self-publishing.

Text messaging and instant communication have changed the way people view information. Lengthy letters were replaced by pithy emails which soon degenerated into abbreviated text messages.

Attention spans grew shorter as people multitasked between all their electronic equipment. Instant messaging, social media updates, news bites in a hundred and forty characters, and even six-second video clips all compete for a slice of a person's active brainwaves.

Books lost mindshare to interactive video games, streaming movies, chat rooms and forums, social networking and blog hopping.

Simply put, people were too busy to read, and the tsunami of books published every week resulted in too many books to read.

Today, many readers read during unexpected downtime, such as waiting at their child's dance lesson, or riding on public transportation. Ebook readers are available on smartphones and tablets, and it is easy to continue reading where you left off.

Longer than a short story, a novella allows readers to identify with the characters, live through a life-changing event, yet complete the story cycle before their attention is torn away by either real life, or the gleaming come-on of another story.

Readers are also less likely to invest days and weeks into a new writer they are unfamiliar with when so many books are begging to be read.

A novel takes too long to get started before an active reader is interrupted, but a novella is paced fast enough to sneak under the reader's initial interest while at the same time ensuring the busy reader that he wouldn't have to wade through reams of material to finish it and get to his next project.

Since novellas get to the meat of the story quicker, are written with a faster pace, are tighter and without superfluous fluff, is it any wonder that novellas are the perfect story form for the 21st century?

Write Shorter

Have you ever waded through a full-length novel and wondered if the story could have been told in half the time?

Have you ever peeked to the end of the book to see if you should wade through multiple subplots and distractions to find the resolution of the main character's dilemma?

If so, you are a prime reader for today's shorter novels and novellas.

A novella is long enough to have character development but does not drag. Modern readers like novellas because there is no bloat, no long wandering subplots, and pages laden with research. A novella is to the point with no sagging middle, long eyeball tiring descriptions and things readers forget about anyway.

Cinematic, action oriented, sound bite, modern, well written novellas are eminently suited for our fast paced world.

The Market for Romance Novellas

The Way Things Were

Romance has always had long forms and short forms. In the old days, when traditional publishers rule the roosts, they had a shorter form called a Category Romance which had to fit in with a delineated set of guidelines. A Category Romance had to fit a certain sized paperback for packaging and shelving purposes and were required to be around fifty to sixty thousand words or two hundred and fifty pages. Beginning romance authors were told to submit for a category line where they had to follow a set of rules and present a uniform reading experience for readers of that category line.

Longer works were called standalone romances and were supposed to be for authors who had busted their chops in Category Romance and were now ready to publish standalone titles. Since paper and printing costs were at a premium, along with transportation costs to ship physical books to bookstores, even standalones were considered to be capped around seventy-five thousand words—more if it was historical, but anything over one hundred thousand words was the "kiss of death."

Ironically, romance stories less than forty-thousand words fared no better. Publishers considered novella length stories to be unpopular with readers because when printed onto a paperback, it appeared too "thin" for the price the publisher wanted to charge the paperback shopper.

The Way Things Are

Fortunately, times have changed and today we have the ebook, or electronic book. Paper and print costs no longer factor into whether a book should be published or not. Readers have also changed and ereading devices are everywhere, on smartphones and tablets. Now, it is possible to carry your entire library in a pocket sized device.

The revolution of ebooks has made word count almost irrelevant. I say almost, because readers still want to know how big of a book they are getting, so publishing sites provide an "estimated" page count either based on the paperback size or a formula computed by the ereader.

But with the advent of ereading and the low prices of ebooks, readers only care about whether they like the stories of a particular author and not how long or short the story is. If an author can keep a reader interested the way Scheherazade did, then the reader will happily buy book after book to keep reading. No trips to the bookstore, no need to donate old paperbacks to the library, no space taken on physical bookshelves or in bulging paper bags under the readers' bed.

What this means is that authors of compelling and interesting books no longer have to "meet" a certain word count or "pad" their books to make a paperback look like a good value, but can focus on telling the story, whether standalone, series, or episodic serial.

This new form of reading and the economics of ebooks favor the author who can write shorter, but still complete stories, that keep the reader coming back for more—much like the One Thousand and One Arabian Nights.

I don't want to belabor this, but simple economics show that if you can write a three book series of stories of forty-thousand words each and sell each book for $4.99, you will make more money than if you put the three books of forty-thousand words into a single tome of three parts and sell it for $9.99.

Not only will your lower price of $4.99 be more attractive to readers, the fact that you have three books as opposed to a single title will give you three hits in the vendor's search engine as opposed to one. You will also be viewed as a more prolific author, and your platform will be larger because you have three "hooks" in the water instead of one. Therefore, the algorithms will favor you with readers who are looking or searching for romances in your category.

Multi-Author Boxed Sets

Now that books are liberated from the costs of paper and ink, many authors are putting together ultra-value-packed multi-author boxed sets to gain new readers. The sets usually include ten or more authors with novels or novellas around a theme, such as Christmas, cowboys, SEALs or paranormal.

Readers of these sets love to sample new authors, and will at least try your book. However, if your story is too long, they may skip to a shorter one because it is easier to finish and they have nine other stories beckoning for their attention.

In a multi-author boxed set, you are offering readers a sample of your work. Therefore you want a complete story that will hook them to your writing. However since you are a new writer for that reader, they may not be motivated or have the patience to plod through a long story, especially if they bought the entire set for 99c.

There are also practical reasons for writing novella length stories for these multi-author boxed sets. In order to price it at 99c, the set must not exceed the file size limit at which a vendor is willing to deliver at 99c.

Secondly, you are going to be dividing the royalties with all the authors of the set, usually an even straight division, so your return on your investment is lower if your story is a lot longer than those of the other authors in the set.

Finally, these sets spring up like wildflowers when a group of authors decide to do one. Your ability to write a novella quickly and efficiently will help you be able to capitalize on joining a set when it comes up. No one wants to wait for the slow plodder after everyone else is finished and ready to upload.

There.

Have I convinced you that writing romance novellas is not only a viable endeavor, but essential if you want to make your mark as a romance author?

Good.

Let's get to the nuts and bolts of writing a romance novella in thirty days or less.

Who Am I?

First, a little bit about myself. I am a self-published romance author who has written and finished over twenty-five complete romance novels and novellas in four years, starting 2012.

I have always dabbled with writing, but before the advent of self-publishing, I was busy managing teams of software developers for a leading networking equipment company. I have a Ph.D. in Applied Mathematics [under my real name] and have made jewelry, mountain dulcimers, and scroll saw crafts as well as playing musical instruments like violin, mandolin, and mountain dulcimers.

Everything changed in 2010 when I realized self-publishing was the grand opportunity for me to turn my writing dreams into reality.

I cut my teeth with an epic historical fantasy, *Michal's Window*, which followed the life of Princess Michal, the wife of King David in the Bible. That book was over a quarter of a million words before I trim, trim, trimmed to what I thought was a manageable

172,500 words. In retrospect, I was stuck in "old" thinking, where I tried to meet publisher guidelines for the size of historical fiction and looked for advice on how many "pages" my book needed to be.

In retrospect, I ended up over-editing it, cutting too much, and I should have kept my words and made this story into a serial of three parts. Anyway, going forward, I published two romance books a year in 2012 and 2013.

In 2014, I realized that the luxury of writing one or two books a year had gone out like cuneiform tablets. Readers wanted new books from their favorite authors immediately, and if I didn't have a new one, they went on to other authors. The top indie writers were churning out books every month in series form or writing serials with cliffhangers.

Because most indie books were sold as ebooks, readers consumed them at a rapid rate, and as long as the author kept them interested, they didn't much care whether it was too long or too short.

Okay, if it was too short, they felt ripped off, but this usually meant not having a complete story, a character arc, and the hallmarks of good writing.

Writing short does not mean taking shortcuts.

In 2014, I wrote and published eight romance novels and novellas, and so far in 2015, I have written fourteen novels and novellas, including a six-book serial.

I'm also the founder of the Romance In A Month method, where I have successfully led over twenty romance authors to write almost one hundred books since May 2014, a year and a half ago from this writing.

My 42,000 word romance, *A Father for Christmas*, was selected in 2015 by Readers' Favorite for a Gold Award in Christmas Romance, and my 85,000 word romantic suspense, *Knowing Vera*, won the 2015 Angie Ovation Awards for best Multicultural Romance.

With that said, let's roll up our sleeves and learn all about writing romance novellas, preferably in thirty days or less.

Novella Structure

Let's begin with story structure.

The structure of a novella is more like a two hour movie than that of an epic novel. In fact, adapting a novel to fit into the confines of a two-hour movie requires the same type of rearrangement and restructuring as writing a novella, which has to have a tighter storyline to traverse the story arc.

While both a novel and a novella can have the traditional three act structure, the novel is a larger story and can take side trips to explore the nuances of the story theme as well as afford several subplots to support the main story.

A novella, like a two-hour movie, has a much tighter structure and does not allow time to explore side avenues and other issues around the plot. Instead, it is focused on the main story problem with the main characters center stage.

One way to experience for yourself the difference between the longer and fuller structure of a novel and that of a novella is to read a novel, then watch the movie right after.

A lot of novel readers say that the movie adaptation changed things from the book, or it cut characters or maybe that it even "ruined" the story. Perhaps this is true, but the movie has to finish in two hours. Therefore the scriptwriter had to rearrange the elements of a novel to fit it into the confines of a movie.

By comparing a full length novel with the movie adaptation, you can easily figure out the essentials that you need to include in your novella and what items you can cut or not write in the first place.

Recently, I read Alice Sebold's *The Lovely Bones*, a full-length novel. Right afterwards, I watched the movie. I was able to immediately identify the simplifications and combinations of plot elements to tighten the novel form of the story to a novella form.

The movie changed the ordering of major events as well as removed subplots that would have required more time to resolve.

Here is my analysis of the differences between the *The Lovely Bones* book versus the movie.

The movie was tighter than the book. The book slows down significantly around the middle where it expounds on the years that go by since Susie, the main character, was murdered, whereas the movie skips this part.

In the book, the action slows when the police are unable to identify Susie's murderer, and Mr. Harvey moves out after Susie's sister snoops in his house and find a drawing of his hole in the ground.

The book then goes on into a subplot about the relationship of Ray and Ruth, Susie's friends. It deals with Ruth questioning her sexuality and exploring it with Ray. It also shows us the dissatisfaction of Ray's mother, Mrs. Singh, with his father being a workaholic and her difficulties in adjusting to the neighborhood, having come from a foreign land. The book also portrays another romance between Susie's sister, Lindsey and her boyfriend Samuel.

The book describes at length how Susie's parents become estranged when her father is obsessed with Mr. Harvey, the murderer, and her mother wants to forget and put things behind her. She ends up having an affair with the investigating detective the night Mr. Harvey slips away from the town.

The movie cut all of this.

Read this again. The movie CUT all of what I just described above. ALL of it. No secondary romances. No friends exploring and reacting to Susie's death. No affair by the mother. No neighbor's marriage problems. None.

The most noticeable thing was that the movie rearranged major events to make the pace faster and the plot more suspenseful. In the book, Mr. Harvey dumps Susie's body in a safe and throws it in the sinkhole shortly after her murder. In the movie, we see him holding onto the safe with the dead body, including a scene where Susie's sister walks right by it when she broke into the house.

The biggest change in the movie is the shortened timeline. Years do not go by. Mr. Harvey does not leave town. Things do not take years to play out. Instead, events are condensed and take place right away, one after the other.

In the book, Mr. Harvey leaves town and the trail goes cold. The book goes on to explore how Susie's death affects so many people: her classmates, her crush, Ray Singh, his family, her father, and of course her sister and brother. The book shows two incidents where Susie's father ends up in the hospital. The first time is when he takes a baseball bat out to the cornfield to attack Mr. Harvey and ends up getting beaten up by a teenage boy who thought he was a stalker.

In the book, the mother goes to the hospital to see the father, but instead has an affair with the investigating police officer. Later, she leaves to go to California and only comes back years later when the father suffers a heart attack.

As I noted earlier, the movie changes all of this. In the movie, the mother leaves when she can't cope. She does not have an affair with the police officer. She's just gone and the comical relief figure of the grandmother moves in.

In the movie, Mr. Harvey does not move away. He sticks around in a menacing way, while Susie's father goes around accusing everyone, including Mr. Harvey.

The movie delays Susie's sister's snooping of Mr. Harvey's house until near the end, and of course, it shows Lindsey walking by the safe that holds Susie's remains.

Finally, the movie uses Susie's father's breakdown with the baseball bat as the impetus for the mother to return to the family. Years did not go by in the movie. Susie's sister did not graduate from college as she did in the book. Instead, she is still in high school and living at home.

The movie shows Lindsey, Susie's sister, finding and holding onto the entire sketch book that Mr. Harvey used as a scrap book, including placing a lock of Susie's hair and her picture. The book, meanwhile dismissed the evidence Lindsey found as only a schematic drawing and not something that would have nailed Mr. Harvey.

Because the movie wanted to finish up in two hours, it could not afford to have the police look into Mr. Harvey's guilt. Therefore, Lindsey withheld the evidence once she realized her parents were back together again and did not show the sketchbook to the police.

In the movie, Mr. Harvey finally disposes of the evidence, the safe with Susie's remains into the sinkhole with the help of a neighbor while Ray and Ruth, Susie's friends watch, not knowing how close she was at that moment. He appears to have gotten away with murder.

In both the movie and the book, the family is reunited and Mr. Harvey meets his end by supernatural means. However the book covered a longer time period [years], whereas the movie was vague on the passage of time.

Using this example, we can see that the following were eliminated when adapting the book to the movie.

1. Duplicate characters compressed. Susie has only one friend in Heaven in the movie, Holly, whereas she has several that she chats with in the book.

2. Subplots eliminated. The mother's affair with the detective. The dynamics in the Singh family. Lindsey and Samuel's romance, how they found an old house they want to renovate after college graduation. The estrangement of Susie's mother with her younger brother. The relationship between Ray and Ruth. All of these were cut.

3. Tightened events. Combined two events of Susie's father in the hospital into one. Cut the length of story time and condensed it. The mother didn't stay away for years, just months. Mr. Harvey didn't move away. The mother left earlier in the story so she could return at the end of the story.

In the movie, we have a very simple three act structure.

1. Susie is murdered.

2. Her family falls apart.

The movie has her mother leaving the family early on. It did not show how long her mother tried to cope.

3. The father and sister are obsessed with Mr. Harvey, but are unable to catch him.

4. The climax comes when Mr. Harvey (who in the movie is still in the neighborhood, but in the book has already moved far away) decides to dump the body that is in the safe because he catches Lindsay snooping around in his house.

In the movie, Lindsay actually obtains more evidence than in the book, but at the climatic moment, when she sees her mother return and the family reunite, she decides against reporting Mr. Harvey to the police which would have restarted the media circus.

The movie and book have the same resolution where an icicle caused by Susie kills Mr. Harvey.

The biggest difference is that the movie is much tighter and follows the traditional hero's journey whereas the book explores and deals with other emotional issues, from Lindsay's growing up under the shadow of Susie's murder, to the brother's emotional problems and resentment of the mother for leaving, and even the issues in Mrs. Singh's marriage to a workaholic. The book shows a complete picture of how Susie's death impacted her entire neighborhood and presents a more realistic closure that allows Susie to finally let go, as life has indeed moved on for all those effected. They will never ever forget her, but each person will have grown and confronted his or her own demons because of having been a part of the community where Susie is murdered.

Neither is better. Both tell a complete story, but in a different context. The movie is more focused on the immediate and shortens the time span of the events, whereas the book shows the long term effects as years go by and Susie's murder remains unsolved.

I hope this exercise is helpful for you in terms of seeing how the same bones of a story can exist in both novel and novella form.

Do this exercise yourself. Watch a movie and read the book, then jot down the things that were either deleted, changed, or tightened in the adaptation.

How to Approach Writing a Novella

Because a novella has to have all of the plot structure of a full-length novel, I suggest laying down a skeleton outline before you start.

I know. I know. I'm not an outliner, and I never follow the trail I lay down for a story once I start writing.

However, the case for preparation is more important when writing a story of twenty to forty thousand words than a longer novel where you and your character can discover the meaning of life and their goals while wandering around the story.

Besides, we're all here because we want to write better stories faster, right?

The way I do it is to break the story down to four parts like a football game with four quarters. In these four quarters, I place seven markers. While writing, I note what I'm doing and see if I'm hitting the seven markers.

Meanwhile, I decide ahead of time who my main character is and what he or she wants desperately. I figure out their outer goals as well as inner motivations and what obstacles they will encounter, mostly emotional at this stage since I don't plot out my scenes ahead of time.

Seven Story Markers

Here are my seven markers.
1. Hook
2. Inciting Incident
3. Lock-In
4. Reversal
5. Dark Moment
6. Climax
7. Resolution

I then divide my target word count into eighths. To make things simple, let's say I want to write a 40,000 word novella. Each eighth is 5000 words.

0 – 5000 words. Introduce main characters, throw in the **hook**, hint at the conflict.

5000-10000 words. **Inciting incident** and **lock-in.** Make sure all supporting characters, i.e. allies and villains, are introduced or at least thought about.

10000-15000 words. Development and adjustment. Main character is learning. Conflict is present but in the background. This is the fun and games portion of the new situation your character finds himself in.

15000-20000 words. **Reversal.** Vital piece of information realized by main character. Things get serious. Main characters are aware of difficulties whereas they could have been clueless before or wandering around.

20000-25000 words. Problems and hurdles get more significant. Things are more difficult for main character and allies.

25000-30000 words. Villain gets upper hand. False victory may occur here with **Dark Moment** either happening at the end of this section, or looming to start in the next.

30000-35000 words. Repercussions of **Dark Moment**. Main character has to decide whether to give up or go forward. After decision is made, or maybe with new piece of information or insight, main character marshals all his or her strength and learning to overcome defeat. Wrap up all secondary story questions except for the main one here.

35000-40000 words. **Climax** and **Resolution**. Main character gains the victory and shows how things have changed.

These word counts are not hard and fast, but they are there for a guideline. If you look at any of my stories, I doubt you will find me exact with any of the plot points. While I'm writing, I may not even know what the **Reversal** is or what the **Dark Moment** looks like. I know there is going to be one, but I can't see that far ahead to tell you what it is.

Instead, I look at my word count and tell myself I have to push the story along toward the next marker.

You, of course, may be a plotter and have all your scenes written out with these guidelines. I'm merely suggesting that you have these markers or have thought about them so that you can write your story with as much forward progress and purpose as you can.

Here are some of my thoughts for each marker.

The Hook

The first one is the hook. The hook to me isn't a big event or something momentous, although it could be. For some stories, there's a dead body at the beginning. I suppose that is as big a hook as anything, but it doesn't really bind your reader emotionally to the main character.

What I'm primarily interested in the beginning is to lay down the main story question in the viewpoint of my main character. I need the reader to care for my main character as well as to understand and see what his or her big problem is.

Give some idea of the main character's background so that the reader can identify with her. Add some inner conflict or show the flaw and hint that she is not satisfied with her life the way it is right now.

Since we are writing a romance, the hook has to be romantic, and the most compelling hook is for your hero and heroine to meet.

Set up the meeting, preferably in the first chapter, while introducing your hero and heroine to the reader. Show them in action, going toward their individual goals, but being interrupted by the appearance of the other.

Here are a few examples. In *Whole Latte Love*, workaholic Carina is presented with the option of rooming with a sexy, delectable, flirtatious barista who is sure to distract her from her goals. In *Taming Romeo*, Evie tries to hide when she spots the boy who got away returning to her restaurant as a hot movie star with his entourage. In *Playing Catch*, sex addicts Jeanine and Kirk meet in the corridor of a hotel as they both try to sneak away from their respective one-night-stands.

Presenting the hook in the first chapter is especially important for a novella because you don't have many words to lay down what is normal for your character like you would in a novel that takes longer to get off the ground.

You want to get the romance established immediately and have the reader fantasizing about what could be. Make sure to show attraction as well as foreshadow conflict. Let the sparks fly on page one and you will have your reader hooked.

Be sure to create a well-rounded character with enough personality and background to grab the reader's interest right away. This means you do not set up a lot of random action such as a car chase or a shooting or a long sequence of action events like at the beginning of a James Bond movie.

The reason has to do with the fact that you don't have many words for the reader to bond emotionally with your character. Watching someone karate chop ten bad guys does not help your reader empathize or even understand why your character is making all those cool moves.

My suggestion for the hook is an emotional dilemma for your character. For a mystery with the dead body at the beginning, you need to show why that dead body is important to your main character within the first chapter.

For a romance, your heroine has a definite goal in mind and is not prepared to fall in love. The appearance of the hero definitely changes things. She's instantly attracted, but rehearses all the reasons why getting involved with him is not a good idea.

The purpose of the hook is to elicit reader curiosity as well as give a hint of the conflicts your character will encounter.

The Inciting Incident

The inciting incident is a plot point that usually happens externally and sets the main character's direction in the story. It is the **call to action** that propels the main character forward.

It could be the main character's first response to the hook, but it could also be something that happens to drag the main character into action.

For a novella, I believe it has to be closely related to the hook. You simply don't have the time to develop a series of external events that happen between the hook and the incident to get the story going.

Since a novella is between 20,000 and 40,000 words, the inciting incident has to happen within the first five to ten thousand words, giving you a few chapters to make this happen.

The initial meet may have sparked attraction, but sometimes, it's not enough to get the hero and heroine together. Maybe they meet on an airplane, but being normal people without stalker tendencies, they part ways.

You must now build on the attraction and either cook up an incident that puts them together, or present new information that throws them on the horns of a dilemma.

Structure the inciting incident as a way to show barriers to their attraction while at the same time moving their story forward. For example, despite their attraction, the hero and heroine find that they are competing for the same job, or discover their families hate each other. Boy meets girl, but there's a complication.

Since the inciting incident changes the direction of the story and forces the characters to go forward in a certain direction, it might be the only time you can get away with a coincidence. After all, something has to start the story rolling.

But beware of relying on more coincidences later on. In a novella, any more chance meetings would smack of author manipulation. You don't have enough room for subplots and other elements to conspire and bring about another coincidence.

In Carina's case in *Whole Latte Love*, after a hard day of apartment hunting, she ends up ringing the bell at Dylan, the barista's apartment building. Coincidence.

Lock-In

The lock-in is an important plot point in a romance, as it basically forces the hero and heroine to work together in the the context of the story. It works with the inciting incident to create conflict while giving the romance a chance to get off the ground.

A romance actually has two storylines—the external and the internal. The external storyline shows the hero and heroine going for their own individual goals, while the internal storyline is the push and pull between attraction and disruption of their external goals while they fall in love without meaning to.

The inciting incident is an external event that pushes the story in the direction to test the character's motivation and expose his or her inner conflict.

The lock-in is in place to prevent the character from taking the easy way out. It is something the character agrees to commit to, despite not wanting to do. The lock-in is the **character's response to the call to action**, or as some describe it, the call-to-action accepted.

In romance it could be the hero and heroine agreeing to work on a project together despite fighting their attraction. Or maybe they have no choice but to work together as they are marooned on a desert island together.

The lock-in commits the hero and heroine to a course of action whether they like it or not. Both the lock-in and the inciting incident should point to conflict and make the reader suspect that the hero and heroine may not get what they want.

While you can argue that there is no difference between the inciting incident and the lock-in, I like to make sure that my novella has both, because it gives an additional conflict to the inciting incident.

A longer novel might get away with a loose call to action followed by meandering circumstances to keep the plot boiling, but a novella needs to move, so locking the characters into the forward movement of the story is important.

The Reversal

The reversal is also known as the midpoint moment, or in James Bell's book, the **mirror moment**. It is roughly smack dab in the center of the story where the character realizes something significant that changes his outlook to the problem in front of him.

In most romances, it is the "could this be love" moment. In action and adventure, it may be the moment when a critical ally betrays the hero and he realizes he is all alone in his quest. In a mystery or suspense it may be a realization that the detective had been looking at the problem all wrong. In character driven stories, the character learns something about himself that spurs him to reconsider all his assumptions about his life up to this point.

As you can see, the reversal marker is very important. It also represents a time of reflection and allows the characters to get his bearing.

Before we get to the reversal, we have a period of discovery. If you look at my word-count guideline, you'll see that there is a chunk of words between the Lock-in and the Reversal without a marker. This is okay because it is the fun and games or discovery and adventure portion of the story. The conflict is there, but in the background and the characters are discovering themselves in their new surroundings.

For romances, it would mean the first date, some fun activities and promise of a possible relationship. I generally do not want my characters to fight too much before the midpoint reversal. This is because I want the reader to feel that this relationship is a possibility. I also want the reader to enjoy the hero and heroine together. Fighting and bickering so early turns me off and makes me feel that these two are better off apart. Of course the reader should be aware of the underlying conflict or reason to keep them apart, even if the characters are enjoying hearts and flowers and first kisses.

In *A Father for Christmas*, Kelly and Tyler enjoy an outing at the Ferry Building as well as tree trimming and kissing even though his underlying PTSD and her criminal past have not been examined. The reader knows the impending doom, but the characters are blissfully taking chances.

Remember, before the midpoint, keep things lighter. In a mystery, the detective is running around interviewing suspects, but hasn't gotten too close to the truth. Perhaps the midpoint reversal is a second murder that shows the detective he's been approaching everything wrong.

In a romance, the couple is enjoying the possibilities or have decided to take a chance in a no-strings relationship to enjoy the present moment without thought of the future. Risky behavior despite inner warnings happen because the attraction is so great. In addition, the relationship is still casual, so each thinks he or she can back out easily.

Because you are writing a novella, you do not have room for a lot of scenes and a lot of running around.

My advice is to keep to a few events, like maybe one date or two, but milk it to the fullest in terms of emotions, body language, description, and feelings communicated.

Don't jump around.

In *Christmas Stray*, a 20,000 word novella, I spent a lot of detail in Juliette and Gabe taking care of Patrick, feeding him, reading to him, roasting chestnuts with him, helping him take a bath and telling him a story, tucking him in and even singing in front of the fire. I showed what a happy family could be like, even though neither Juliette nor Gabe believed they could have one. I held off the major conflicts until the Reversal moment to establish that this couple had the potential to succeed.

Too many times, I see authors introducing too much conflict before the midpoint reversal. It gets to the point that the reader wishes the couple would just split up and be done with it.

Although I shouldn't talk, since in *Playing Without Rules*, Marcia and Brock had a lot of conflict before the midpoint reversal, but they were also really good together in bed, and have a past history of loving each other. In any case, I tempered their conflict with loving gestures and an awesomely romantic fishing trip before the reversal.

The Dark Moment

The forces that will ruin the main character's life take on a larger role after the midpoint. This third quarter is where the struggles intensify and the villain or conflict escalates.

Because the stakes are higher, your character is likely to over react and make mistakes. These mistakes all feed into the conflict and help the villain.

In most romances, the forces that should keep the couple apart, in addition to their own insecurities and fear of commitment, escalate out of control and lead to the dark moment.

Even though I put this moment at the 75% marker, I tend to make it later for my own romances because I need more time to build the case, by showing instead of telling, that the couple in question have the love, the skills, the abilities, and determination to solve the problem themselves.

During this time, the villain or forces that would keep them from succeeding are gaining momentum, and this is a good time to show your characters struggling as well as committing in their mind that the relationship is worth fighting for despite their fears.

For action and adventure stories, you might even move the Dark Moment earlier because your character needs more time to prepare for the final fight. There is also the chance for a false victory right before a deeper, darker moment. This false victory can give everyone, including the reader, a temporary respite from the increasing tension.

But, as I said before, I personally like to push the Dark Moment closer to the end and wrap up the Climax and Resolution quickly.

Others may not agree with me, but I feel energy is lost once the Dark Moment hits, because the worst has happened, and since I feel like I've made the case earlier why my couple should be together, I don't have them wallowing endlessly in tears and depression.

Instead, the person who caused the rift makes an effort to show the other person why he or she should reconsider, and because the underlying love is still there, my couple usually get to their Climax and Resolution fairly close to the Dark Moment.

I'm mentioning this because in a novella, I don't have as many words to work with, and for me, I'd rather skip over the wallowing part which typically involves the guy drinking himself into a stupor and the girl crying her eyes out with all her girlfriends.

This time period is good for self-reflecting and gives the protagonist a chance to figure out what went wrong. You can also use this moment to close out any dangling subplots such as estranged relationships, clean up any external conflict, and prepare the protagonist for the climax where she confronts and resolves her greatest fears and internal conflict.

Your mileage may vary and I'm not saying what I do is right. The important thing is to do what's right for your story and make sure every action is well motivated and comes about believably through a chain of cause and effect.

Climax

The Climax shows the main character gaining victory over his enemies and earning mastery over his internal conflict. It is the crowning moment for the entire story. Spend enough time at the climax and really milk it for all it's worth.

If it's a fight scene, show it in great detail. I won't give away *Knowing Vera's* climatic fight scene, but it is shown in almost slow motion, with every action and detail described.

The Climax in most romances is the Grand Romantic Moment. It is the final reunion and the reward for readers. Because novellas are short, you should try to make it memorable and stage it well. In both *Playing the Rookie* and *Played by Love*, the heroine stages the final Grand Romantic Moment elaborately, including a love scene.

A physical love scene is not necessary if the main energy of the story points to an emotional breakthrough. In this case, have your characters discuss their emotional breakthrough to fully appreciate that they've gained a new level of intimacy. Again, spend your words wisely and make each of the marker scenes full and rich.

Obviously in a detective story, the climax is the unveiling of the crook with all of the excitement of the trap or capture. Again, don't shortchange the climax. Spend the words necessary to make sure it feels complete and fulfilling to the reader.

Resolution

The resolution solves the story problem. While I don't believe you should shortchange the resolution, I do think it could be an area where if possible, you can finish it off with a few paragraphs or even a line or two.

This depends on how well you resolved all of the minor open issues before the Climax. If you've taken care of everything before the Climax, it is possible to finish off with a few sweet words.

However, if your Climax was shorter and more succinct, a longer resolution is needed to convince the reader that things indeed ended satisfactorily.

At this stage, you might be overrunning your word count and be tempted to cut things short. A word of warning. Don't.

Complete the circle and show that the initial story problem is solved. Show your characters happily ever after, or if you're leaving a cliffhanger, make sure it is adequately set up and not cut off abruptly.

Tips for Effective Novellas

Limit Subplots

This is the common advice on writing a novella. Some say a novella should have no subplot. This is simplistic and subject to debate.

The subplot exists to give additional dimension to the characters and their struggles. It enriches the plot and allows layers of meaning to be added to the theme.

Because we want our novellas to be as rich and nuanced as our longer novels, I'm afraid that truly limiting a novella to a single plot could cause some of the problems people have with the novella form.

For example, cardboard characters, or lack of character motivation, or predictable plot is a typical complaint for stories the reader feels are too short or not satisfactory.

One way to increase the complexity of a novella without adding a full-fledged subplot is to create a secondary hook to keep the reader's interest and deepen the characters at the same time.

A secondary hook can be a suspense element, or a secondary goal that the main character must achieve besides his or her primary one. For example, in a romance the primary goal is for the hero and the heroine to love each other forever after or for now. A secondary goal could be getting a promotion, winning a contest, earning a degree, and of course solving a mystery, or staying out of danger.

Secondary goals enrich the characterization as well as create more opportunities for plot twists. Whether the main character achieves the secondary goal or maybe changes his or her mind at the end, the process of struggling for that goal keeps the novella from being on a single-track or being too predictable.

In *A Father for Christmas*, even though the main story is Kelly and Tyler's love story, secondary goals include both of them getting jobs they are happy with, and of course, Kelly's daughter Bree getting her Christmas wish come true is also important to the story.

Limit Locations

Another way to keep the novella rich while saving words is to keep the setting in the same place as much as possible. Don't move your characters from here to there, across town, across the country, or around the world.

Each time you move your characters, you must describe the setting in sufficient detail to ground your reader into the reality of your fictional dream. If you are writing science fiction, you must include sufficient world building for each civilization or planet your character lands on.

Successful novellas can be written in the same small town among locations familiar to the reader, such as schools, offices, and stores.

Another way to limit word count is to use familiar contemporary locations with a warm, family and community feel. For example, when you write a Christmas novella, use common Christmas customs and traditions that readers are familiar with, e.g. tree trimming, visiting Santa, tree lighting, caroling, etc.. Obviously you should avoid being too cliché, but staying in a small town or familiar setting will help you keep your descriptions tight.

Another thing to keep in mind is to cut driving scenes or scenes where characters travel from one place to another. End scenes earlier and start scenes later, using jumps with a short summary to ground the reader. But, beware of talking heads or leaving the reader to wonder where the characters are. Include two or more senses in each scene: sight, sound, scent, taste, or touch.

The easiest is to not change locations or introduce too many locations. For example, *Christmas Stray* takes place entirely in the vicinity of the rented cabin in the mountains.

Tighter Timeframes

A novella is not well suited to multi-year stories that encompass large spans of time. While it is not as short as a short story, which might take place within the same day or in a few hours, it is better to keep your novella's timeframe within a few days or at most a few weeks timeframe.

If your story spans a few weeks, make sure to use time jumps and summarization. For example: *The next few weeks they settled into a routine of dinner and dates, although avoiding the subject of his impending deployment.*

Keeping to one linear thread in time makes it easier for you to tell your story without having to go back and remind the reader what happened in a different timeline. Rather than jumping back and forth in time, or going into flashback mode, or two time tracks, one in the present the other in the past, keeping the novella moving in the present makes it easy to follow. Leave fancy framing devices to novels where there is more time and space to orient and reorient the reader.

Ironically, because you have less words to develop characters and events, you must actually spend more time and words on the crucial events to draw out its importance. So while you summarize between scenes, you must do complete scenes when your characters are on stage. Otherwise, your reader will never feel grounded, and your story will be too choppy.

Writer fewer scenes, but make sure they are full-length scenes.

Do not fall into the trap of several short scenes jumping from one place or time to another. I've seen this done by inexperienced writers, and I feel like I'm reading a plot synopsis.

Don't do that.

Fewer Characters

Decide on your main characters and a minimum list of supporting characters and villains. Instead of a large group of friends, concentrate on one best friend. Instead of involving the entire extended family, bring in one or two main family members.

Make sure each character has a purpose or multiple purposes.

A novella will generally deal with one or two important relationships instead of multiple intertwining relationships.

At the same time, limit the number of point of view characters. Each point of view character must be developed fully and be well rounded.

I would suggest no more than two point of view characters in a novella.

Deep Motivation

Perhaps the biggest weakness of the novella form is inadequate motivation. The writer has decided what the story is supposed to be about and simply moves the characters through the plot like puppets.

There is a lot of action but not enough motivation and a lack of emotions. This happens when characters are made to do things because a certain plot point or marker is reached. Because the characters have not been fully developed, the reader fails to believe the character would actually do what he is assigned to do.

The way to fix this is to fully develop your character's goals, motivation, and internal conflict, before letting them move around taking action.

I've read novellas where a character's belief system changes so suddenly I have whiplash. The writer created a character, but because the story was short, she did not have room or adequate story time to develop the character. She simply had the character do a one-eighty near the end of the story and do something she swore she would never do.

I'm sure you've read stories like that and they are disappointing. Writing a novella is no excuse. You must still present rich characters with internal conflict and deep motivation. Your characters must change in a believable way, tested by the events of the story as well as his or her own actions. You cannot "make" your character do something because you must have a plot point, such as it's time for a love scene so my character suddenly goes against her deeply held beliefs and jumps the bones of the next man she meets.

I feel like I'm repeating myself again, but no jumping around, no jumping conflict, and no heaping problems and trouble on your character, piling it all on and then magically having them solve everything very quickly.

There are certain events and scenarios that almost always require deeper investigation and more time for the characters, as well as the reader, to fully process. Examples are death late in the story, serious injury late in the story, and in my opinion, anything dealing with child abuse, rape, and violent death.

It is extremely difficult to write these traumatic events and backstory into a novella and do justice to your characters.

Even the classic, sick or injured and almost death to "make" the hero or heroine realize how much they'll miss the love interest may cause eye-rolling when shoved in near the end of the novella. You lose the reader any time she suspects you are using a plot device to finish off the story.

My belief is that it's more effective if you have more story time to deal with the consequences of a death of a close family member or a serious injury of the love interest than throwing it in at the end and resolving it quickly.

That's why I would almost want to say that a novella deals with "lighter" fare: Christmas wishes, second chances, and holiday romances. I'm not saying it can't be done, but saving a woman from being held as a sex slave and having the story end with feeding each other wedding cake in forty-thousand words seems like a big stretch.

This bears repeating. Fewer events, fewer scenes, but each scene as rich as in a full-length novel.

Never, ever make your character do something because the marker says something should happen at that moment. If whatever you plotted or planned beforehand doesn't fit yet, take your time to develop your characters until it does. Don't rush your plot markers.

And please, don't rush a love scene. Wham, bam, thank you ma'am, went out of style a long, long time ago. It is better to fade to dark if you want to save the words, than to stick A into B, huff and puff a few times, and blow the house apart all in a single paragraph.

Writing a novella does not mean rushing through scenes and orchestrating unbelievable actions. It simply means same character development, same motivation, same richness in description and setting, but less events and detours and development of secondary characters.

Each moment in your novella deserves to be rich enough to be in a full-length novel. Remember that and take it to the bank.

Let it be a Novel

Lastly, if your story deserves more time and has more conflict and development than fitting inside of 40,000 words, then let it be a novel. Why limit yourself? Don't let word count dictate your story, but give each story the number of words it needs. Nothing more and nothing less.

Novella Genres

What genres are suited for novellas? Romance, short mysteries, westerns, Christmas and holiday stories

Mysteries [lighter than murder, young adult mystery, theft, cheating, missing object]

A short adventure, an outing, a vacation.

Young adult story about an event such as the prom, homecoming, or football championship game, or a class.

Suspenseful snack, stalking, crime, make it intense but fast.

Sci-fi, fantasy, doable even with a short amount of world building

Bridge story to a series, prequel to a series.

Sub-characters getting their own story, maybe a wedding story or a holiday story.

Link your novellas to a concept, pets, a single location, a group of people, a tour group, a band of thieves, a linked set of sports stories.

Romance Tropes Suited for Novellas

Since I write mostly romance, I have some thoughts about the tropes most suited to novellas. Many people don't like instant love in romances. However in a romance novella, instant love is okay if you prepare it right. Start by showing the hero and heroine as having their best day ever. They are instantly attracted, or maybe have been set up for a dream date. You don't have time for your couple to play cat and mouse, or to throw a lot of complications before they get together. Don't feel compelled to make a case for why the hero and heroine are attracted to each other. They just ARE.

Tropes which work well for novella format are: Instant Love, Second Chance, Vacation Affair, Reunion stories, i.e. Crush from the Past.

Instant Love and Vacation Affair start with the mindset that both the hero and heroine are throwing caution to the wind in embarking in a fun and light-hearted love affair. Complications set in later, but at the beginning, all is hearts and flowers.

Second Chance and Reunion stories have the advantage that there is history between the hero and heroine. They already know each other and were attracted in the past or had a relationship. This familiarity means it is more believable that they might start something up again despite the problems that kept them apart.

Tropes which are more difficult include: Friends to Lovers, something has to change to trigger the romantic feeling between two people who have been friend-zoned for so long. Family Feud or Forbidden Love involves either family or other external obstacles and people. More needs to be overcome. Same with Opposites Attract. Not saying these are impossible, and in fact, I urge you to try writing a novella with these tropes. But keep in mind that you will have a higher hurdle to overcome in terms of believability.

Writing a Novella in Two Weeks

Day 1

Pick a story out of your bucket list. Make sure it has a straightforward goal. Novellas are like running straight down the middle of the field.

Can the problem be solved in a one hour TV drama? Or will it require a full length movie?

Write your tagline. Write a sample description. 20 words, 50 words, 100 words. Make sure it it is clear.

Start your tagline with the story question and expand.

Will X get Y?

Sketch your seven markers. You don't have to know all of them, but you should at least have your Hook, Inciting Incident, and some thought about the Lock-In.

Set placeholder for the events that will show each of the markers.

Day 2

Character sketches. List main goal and main conflict between the main characters. List two subordinate goals.

List main motivation and two subordinate motivations.

Brainstorm all conflict areas. Be wild and crazy. Don't worry whether these will make it into the final story.

Look for pictures of your characters on the internet.

List one positive trait, one flaw, one quirk

What is the main personality type of your character?

Feel free to change the markers to fit your character.

Day 3

Prepare to write. You can write in any order. Some people write linearly, others jot things down and fill in. Some write the ending.

Divide your "target" word count by 10. Whereas usually I don't sweat word count, I do when writing a novella.

This is because your first indication that you've gone into the weeds is if you are exceeding your word count at each target.

Aim for 12-20 chapters. Or three to five chapters per quarter. List events that need to happen and roughly fit them into the chapters.

Jot down the milestones you want to hit. You can do this all at once beforehand, or list them for each quarter or eighth as you get there. For the purposes of the schedule, I'll assume you are writing in order.

Day 4

Write 1/10 of your total word count each day. For example, if you're aiming for 20,000 words, write 2000 words today.

The first 10% of your story must include the **Hook**. If writing a romance, put in a scene where your hero and heroine meet. Introduce characters, allies, comical moments, and a hint of conflict to hook your reader.

Also make sure you show your characters working actively toward one of their external goals. Now is a good time to show the initial attraction between hero and heroine—the spark and promise of a romance. [10%]

Day 5

Today, you will end at 20% of your story. Build from the hook and move your characters toward the Inciting Incident which happens at 25%.

Plant the seeds of conflict now. See if you can let the reader know that even though your hero and heroine are attracted to each other, it's not all smooth sailing ahead. Continue to introduce characters, allies, villains, situations and foreshadowing for future conflict and resolution. Include a small steamy moment, like the first kiss, to establish the attraction and desire between hero and heroine. [20%]

Day 6

The **Inciting Incident** or **Call to Action** will happen roughly halfway in today's word count. Show the transition from the "ordinary" world to the "story" world. Something has drawn your hero and heroine into this romantic journey.

Today is the day to lock them in together—to show why they will continue to work together. Put them in a situation where they will come into frequent contact with each other, and don't forget the conflict. [30%]

Day 7

From 30% to 40%, you are in the rising action portion, the "fun and games" time of the romance where attraction is new and the hero and heroine are setting aside their differences, at least on the surface, and instead are getting to know each other. Explore how they are together. Let them ignore potential problems and enjoy each other, but keep the conflict simmering in the background.

Use today's word count to show WHY your hero and heroine are perfect for each other. Attraction should be there, and they can't keep their hands off each other. They might both try and act casual about it even if they get physical.

You might also introduce a secondary plotline to show your reader why your characters are likeable and deserve a happy ending. Pets and small children are very useful in this respect. [40%]

Day 8

March to the **Midpoint**. At the end of the day, you will be at 50%. After the fun and games and the initial harbingers of conflict, the romance takes a serious turn when one or both of the characters realize they could possibly fall in love—that this is serious. The moment when everything changes is the **midpoint reversal**. Maybe it had been all for fun before, or a fake relationship, but a change happens that forces your characters to reflect on whether this relationship is life-changing or not. New information is available and this time, if they get physical, it means a lot more than before. [50%]

Day 9

Now that the romance is important and serious, the underlying conflicts become fraught with meaning. Problems and hurdles cause doubt between one or the other. Show the escalation of tension, worry, and let the villains make their move. Things don't look that rosy, but don't forget to show what victory "could" look like, so that your reader roots for the romance to work. [60%]

Day 10

Tension and conflict escalate, but at the same time, you should include another interlude of passion and affection to show what could be lost if things don't work out. Again, a good place for the subplot to reveal more about your hero and heroine's characters—show them to be basically good people, maybe damaged, but ultimately redeemable and deserving of each other and a happy ending. This is the last chance to establish their basic character traits before the tumultuous events of the dark moment and climax end the story. [70%]

Day 11

Today's writing includes the 75% mark: the **Dark Moment** or the **Big Bad Breakup**. The relationship is severely tested and at a breaking point. The villain has the upper hand, and the romance is at its darkest point.

I typically delay my Dark Moment to the last 20% of the story, so I might have a "false victory" here, where hero and heroine paper over their differences and attempt to make a compromise that the reader knows will not work. They are tempted to take the easy way out, but of course, this blows up in their faces.

But whichever way it turns out, both hero and heroine are apt to make mistakes or say or do something they might regret. Just don't make it too unredeemable. Now also might be a good time for a very tempestuous love scene. [80%]

Day 12

The romance is in jeopardy and because both the hero and heroine are in love, even if they don't admit it, the breakup causes each of them to question everything they assumed. They retreat to their corners and lick their wounds, but not for long.

Because this is a novella, you don't have pages and pages to describe their despair, depression, drunkenness or endless tears. You only have a few thousand words to get the romance back on track.

This is the time for your characters to either seek counsel, or dig deep into their inner strengths and overcome whatever conflicts or obstacles that had been holding them back.

Wrap up all subplots at this point. New information may come to light and both hero and heroine separately realize their relationship is worth fighting for.

Take some time for tears and counsel, but don't overdo it. Focus on fixing problems and showing your characters' strength and proactiveness. Either show the **Climax** or **Grand Romantic Moment** today, or build up to it for tomorrow. [90%]

Day 13

The **Climax** or **Grand Romantic Moment** happens today, along with the **Resolution** or **Happily Ever After**.

Show the hero and heroine making their way back to each other. Their differences are settled and they rebuild their relationship, realizing that they could not live without the other.

Once the Hero and Heroine have made up and declared their love, show the happy resolution so that the reader gets some of the afterglow.

Because a novella is short, you might jump a few months or a length of time and end with a short Epilogue showing a time in the future to assure the reader that all is well in the long term. [100%] **THE END!**

Note: Even though I'm telling you approximately where your markers are in terms of word count, I don't want you to stick to it too closely or worry about the exact percentages. These guidelines are to help you stick to the story structure or stay as close as you can. If your word count goes over, don't worry about it. Maybe your story was meant to be longer. In any case, you can edit later.

Day 14

Read over your novella and fill in any places that you skipped ahead, round out the descriptions, strengthen the characters.

Congratulations! You're done. Set it aside, then revise it before sending to your editor or beta reader.

Case Study (Christmas Stray)

In January 2015, I wrote *Christmas Stray*, a 20,000 word novella, within forty-eight hours.

Did I do everything I recommended? Maybe, but I didn't compute word counts or anything. What I did was dream up almost the entire story in my mind, minus the details, and then I started writing. I knew I had to get to the **Lock-In** event relatively quickly, so I made sure they were snowed in. There, no escape.

Actually, let me backtrack. I cheated. I started with a couple who already had a background. They knew each other and were already in love. In fact, they were married but unfortunately on the verge of divorce. They decided to get away to a remote mountain cabin to repair their marriage.

The **Hook** was apparent on the first page. The protagonist, Juliette, gets pissed off at a Christmas tree. Wow. Who attacks a Christmas tree? I immediately show her conflicted emotions. She's grieving for a son who died of leukemia the day before Christmas a year ago. She doubts that she can repair her marriage, but she's willing to give it one last shot because she still loves her husband, Gabe.

The **Inciting Incident** happens in Chapter 2. Juliette and Gabe find a stray dog and a six-year-old boy hiding behind the woodpile. The **Lock-In** follows immediately. They are snowed in the next morning and the car is iced up, and they can't open the doors to get their cell phones. I then compound their problems by cutting off the electricity.

Now the entire cast of characters are stuck together, snowed in, and without power in a remote cabin. They are forced to make do, and to interact with each other.

The first half shows Juliette reeling in grief and not responding well to her husband's overtures. She's making them miserable, but for the sake of the child they have good times. They roast chestnuts, read to the child, play with the dog, but the conflict between Juliette and Gabe escalates under the surface.

The midpoint **Reversal** is reached by Chapter 6. At the end of Chapter 5, Gabe has decided to separate from Juliette and go for the divorce. One of my beta readers said this was the earliest ever in a story to have the tears start.

The **Reversal** happens when Juliette realizes she is the cause of their problems, whereas earlier she was blaming Gabe. It's precipitated by a mini crisis where the puppy runs off and they set off to find him. They find the puppy under a fir tree that the child declares to be the perfect Christmas tree. Uh oh.

Remember the **Hook**? Juliette did not want a Christmas tree. Suffice it to say, this sets off her withdrawal and during that time, she begins to realize that she is the one ruining everything.

From there, we have an accelerated series of attempts and backtracks as Juliette and Gabe dance around their feelings. However, there is a difference. This is the second half, where the protagonist, Juliette, has knowledge and is working her way back. In this case, Juliette is now trying to make overtures to Gabe and he has withdrawn, having already made the decision to proceed with the divorce.

Now the ball is in her court. Again we have scenes with the child, tree trimming, bath time story and then another mini crisis, a fire in the garage that ends in another confrontation with her husband where he refuses her attempt at seduction.

I didn't time it my story or count words, seriously, but when I went back to evaluate it, the **Dark Moment** was exactly at 75%.

Once her husband rejects her underhanded way of getting him back, Juliette has to face the truth and make real change. This happens in Chapter 9 out of 12.

In Chapter 10, Juliette fixes Christmas Eve breakfast and the four of them enjoy a wonderful day. This leads to the **Climax** which is Christmas morning, when the power comes back on and ... Well, I'm not going to give the story away.

Discoveries are made and from there the story ends in a bittersweet manner. Juliette and Gabe are together and return home with a special gift, vowing to return every year to their Miracle Cabin.

My writing schedule happened like this. On Sunday night, I wrote the first chapter and part of the second chapter showing the state of the marriage. It starts with the hook, the rejection of a Christmas tree, and ends in a stalemate—Juliette goes to bed with her husband. (1800 words)

The next day, Monday, I breezed through the entire first half of the book and into part of the second half, from the inciting incident to the midpoint reversal and into part of the recovery phase. Chapters 2-7 (roughly 10200 words).

The story was still brewing in my head and every time I would go upstairs to go to sleep, I'd jot down something I thought up. On Tuesday, I went walking with my friend in the morning, obviously talking about my story, and then wrote the rest of the 8000 words, finishing in the evening, and well within 48 hours of my start for a total of 20,000 words.

Because I'm a pantser, I didn't note the markers where I said, "this has to happen, and that has to happen." I didn't even know what event I was going to use for each of the markers.

Admittedly, I knew the **Lock-In** was the power outage and iced up car. But the midpoint **Reversal** 50% and **Dark Moment** 75% mark seemed to follow naturally. I was aware of them, but did not plan for them, unlike my recommendations above.

You might work differently, of course, and it's always good to jot down what you think those markers should be to keep yourself on track.

Will I always be able to write a novella in 48 hours? I doubt it, but *Christmas Stray* was a perfect storm, and I'm pretty happy with how it turned out.

The key points

I started with a couple who knew each other already. Second Chance romance works faster than Love at First Sight where you have to establish the basis for a couple to be attracted and then decide to pursue a relationship.

I created a tight **Lock-In**. What could be tighter than being snowed in or marooned together?

I threw in a catalyst (**Inciting-Incident**) to stir their feelings. An orphan boy and a stray dog. The entire situation tugs at the heart and helps them see the good in each other despite their conflicts.

The remote location and being snowed in allowed for crisis situations to drive toward a milestone. This is external conflict pushing the characters to expose their internal conflict.

Finally, Christmas is an emotional holiday and one where people try to create good times. It can also be a time of family confrontation. The backdrop of the holidays allowed me to push the timeline. Christmas is coming. The clock doesn't stop.

In the end, my characters go back to the normal world, i.e. home. They are changed and transformed by their experience at the remote mountain cabin.

Step-by-Step Guide

In May-June 2015, I ran a class on writing a Quickie Romance Novella in my Romance In A Month group on Facebook. Here are the slides that will lead you step-by-step through my method of writing a romance novella. Even to this date, I still use the character definition questions whenever I start a new story and I check through the exercises and plot points before revising my first draft.

https://www.facebook.com/groups/romanceinamonth/

What is a Novella?

- A Novella is shorter than a novel and longer than a short story. (20,000 to 40,000 words)
- Long enough for a reader to immerse in a world and feel for the characters.

- Short enough to be read in one or two sittings.
- Novella is a complete story with three act structure.

The Novella Form

- A sonata in music with three acts: exposition, development, recapitulations
- A one-hour TV drama: four acts, corresponding to the commercial breaks at each quarter hour.
- A fairy tale: illustrates a single theme with a small cast of characters, easily digested, but intense and complete

Neither Here Nor There

- Novellas are often defined by what they're not, not what they are.
- Sandwiched between short story and full-length novel.
- Traditional publishers hated them because they couldn't charge $25 for a hardback nor could magazines bundle them like they do with shorts.

- Stephen King called the novella "an ill-defined and disreputable literary banana republic"

Exercise #1

- Why do you read novellas?
- Why do you want to write a novella?
- What questions do you have about writing a novella versus a novel?

Novella Opportunities

- New Generation of Readers live in a world of instant messaging, video clips, and tweets – short reader attention span.
- Ebook publishing and low prices means no price pressure for larger and longer books.
- Today's TV and movie watching reader no longer require long descriptions to visualize a scene.

Writing Short Doesn't Mean Bad Writing

- Cutting Corners on Story Structure
- Cardboard Characters

- Loose Ends
- Clichéd Writing – formula, predictable
- Lack of Story Arc and Conflict
- Low or No Character Growth
- Low or No Stakes
- Telling and not Showing
- Lack of adequate backstory

Exercise #2

- Think back on some novellas you've read.
- What did the author miss?
- What frustrated you?
- List your peeves, so we can avoid them.

A Model Novella

- *A Christmas Carol* by Charles Dickens
- Identifiable main character: Scrooge
- Flawed to allow for change: miserly, no Christmas spirit
- Three Testing Events: Three Spirits
- Subplot to illustrate transformation: Bob Crachit and his family, Tiny Tim
- Backstory, shown by Sprit of Past

A Novel to a Movie == Novella

- When screenwriters make a movie out of a novel, they have to cut and streamline. Tighten the plot, combine characters.
- How many times have you read the book, watched the movie, and noticed all the things missing?
- Think about a book that was made into a movie. What was changed?

Compact Storyline Starter

- Complex Characters + Focused Conflict = Clear Change
- Character is always important – even in Flash Fiction. Reader must always identify or want to follow a character.
- Focused Conflict – rifle point instead of shotgun. Conflicts must be relevant to making characters change.
- Clear Change – demonstrated at the end with characters and theme.

Character Definition

- Easily understood backstory

- Recent wound or flaw
- What does she want?
- What does change look like for her?
- Identify the theme right now
- What types of conflict will stymie her?
- What does she wish for more than anything? How can she accomplish?

Exercise #3

- Create your characters.
- Answer the Character Definition Slide bullets for your heroine and your hero. Optionally, if you already know of a villain or ally, do a summarized version for them also.
- Think about what a resolution looks like for your character's flaws and wounds.

Seven Story Milestones

- Hook – Something about Character that causes reader to want to find out more.
- Inciting Incident – Cute Meet
- Lock-in – Core Conflict Magnified
- Midpoint – Oops, I'm in Love
- Dark Moment – Big, Bad Breakup
- Climax – Grand Romantic Moment

- Resolution – Happily Ever After

The Hook

- Very Important. Without it, reader will put book down, or not buy it when reading the 10% sample online.
- Goal: get the reader to care about both your character and his/her dilemma.
- Fulfill a reader need: for mystery, laughs, promised romance, problem to solve, culture to learn about, thrills, horrors – answer to why they picked up the book.

Hook Depends on Genre

- Mysteries often start with a body
- Thrillers start with the point of view of the unknown or creepy villain perhaps spying on the innocent victim to be
- Fantasy paints the magical realm
- Young Adult starts in the internal world of the main character, usually first person point of view.
- Romance starts with potential love interest or promise of love

Exercise #4

- Brainstorm and jot down several possible hooks.
- Ask a few friends if the hooks make them feel curious and intrigued
- Have them guess how the story would turn out based on the hook.

Romance First Page

- Some people insist both hero and heroine MUST appear on the first page together.
- I don't agree because that is a "rule" and can become a cliché.
- First page's goal is to hook the reader by dangling a promise. If you read this, you'll feel like this. Will it be funny? Or poignant? Or exploratory? What is the reason to keep reading?

Hero and Heroine on First Page Pros

- Strong start, if you can quickly get readers to care about them while on stage together.

- Fulfills promise that there will be a romance. Gives reader opportunity to check out both hero and heroine and immediate see the potential for both love and conflict.
- Recommended if you're a beginner.

Hero and Heroine on First Page Cons

- No opportunity to allow reader to bond with heroine and hero before they are on stage together.
- No opportunity to show hero and heroine in their "normal" world before running into this potential love interest. Some romances start with one chapter of the heroine and one chapter of the hero before they come together. There's usually a hint or foreshadow of the potential love story to drive interest.
- With less background on characters, reader is watching people she doesn't care about flirt or argue on their first meet.

First Meet – Inciting Incident

- Whether on page one or not, should be before 10%-12%
- Must show: attraction, spark, memorable moment, and foreshadow conflict
- First chance to have hero describe heroine and heroine describe hero – make it count.
- Effect: both hero and heroine walk off thinking about the other

Exercise #5

- Brainstorm the First Meet
- How do you show the spark of attraction? Why does your character take notice?
- Conversation, dialogue is important. Do not narrate. Show in action.
- Any surrounding characters, allies, possible antagonists? What is the location and venue? What happens next?

Reaction to First Meet

- What is the Hero and Heroine's separate reaction?
- Show Push/Pull between Attraction and Conflict
- Explore potential conflict, but don't overdo it.
- Show Flirtation, Plans for date or get-together. Internal fantasies and daydreams – OR - show resistance and doubt overcome by attraction

Exercise #6

- Write a scene that shows their attraction. What do they like about each other?
- How do they try to find out about each other?
- Have you shown how they can't keep their hands off each other?
- How do their internal thoughts contrast with the external action?

Fun and Games

- Let them enjoy themselves. Show reader why they are perfect for each other, despite their wounds and internal conflict.
- Remind reader of looming problem, even if hero and heroine are oblivious and enjoying themselves.
- Throw in a monkey wrench, either enemy, ticking time bomb, or bad situation. Show how H/h react.
- Sensual scenes more physical than emotional. Lust, fun, excitement.

The Lock-in and Core Conflict

- Happens at approximately 25% of story.
- Think of one or more major reasons why Hero/Heroine should NOT be together. This is your core conflict.
- Now, lock them into the story together, so they cannot split and leave.
- Both want but cannot have. Example: Family feud (conflict), crush or secretly in love (lock-in)
- Do not want but forced together. Example: Dislike or "not my type"

(conflict), forced to work together (lock-in)

Exercise #7

- What is the Core Conflict?
- Did you hint at it earlier? A tiny foreshadow?
- How will you show it looming now that the hero and heroine are "locked-in?"
- How does the Core Conflict push and pull with the Attraction or Trope situation H/h are intertwined together in?

Raise Emotional Stakes

- Increase reader empathy with hero and/or heroine. Helping someone in need. Defending the weak. Sticking to a principle. Sacrifice for honor or duty.
- Let reader be aware of vulnerability, secret wishes, desires to overcome wound. Baby steps in learning to trust hindered by doubts and insecurity.
- Show passion and desire moving from purely physical to emotional.

Exercise #8

- What is the dominant emotion motivating your characters' lives?
- Do not rely entirely on lust, limerance, and romantic emotions.
- Well rounded characters have other things going on in their lives: job searches, competitions, family situations, and other events that cause emotions.

Help I'm in Love - Midpoint

- Realization this is serious! Stakes increase.
- This time is different. This could be the once in a lifetime love.
- Despite looming conflict, growing love (even when unacknowledged) causes H/h to take risks and forge ahead.
- Love Scene appropriate, passionate but emotional and special, but not fully there, still holding back.

Exercise #9

- Write a scene that shows one or both characters' "uh oh" moment of wondering if he or she is in love, or knowing it.
- What is his or her reaction?
- Does it cause problems? If so, show it.
- What risks do they take?
- How is their relationship different now with the increased stakes of being "in love?"

Foreshadow Dark Moment

- Emotional scene from the midpoint exposes potential conflict that will test this couple to the extreme
- Show opposition and how H and h might respond, together and separately.
- Increase emotional stakes, now that they are in love and are aware of the opposition.

Show Basis for True Love

- Don't forget to remind your readers WHY H/h should be together.

- Create a scene that shows how good they are to each other, despite the brewing conflict.
- Calm before the storm. Let H/h enjoy some lighthearted fun before big conflict guns come out.
- Show what Victory can be like

Exercise #10

- How are you magnifying the conflict while still showing that the H/h are meant to be together?
- Have you resolved subplots? Try not to dangle them too long or they interfere with your ending.
- Write a scene that shows how good they can be together, if only their internal flaws can be resolved.

Dark Moment

- Approx 75% - 80%
- Love is tested and internal flaws are exposed. Cannot hide anymore. Truth must come out.
- Make this big and directly related to the wounds and flaws you worked on

earlier—not a mere misunderstanding that a phone call would resolve.

- Both hero and heroine lose something worthwhile. Don't make it one-sided.

Reeling and Recovering

- Show the effect of the breakup or crisis on the hero and the heroine.
- How do they react?
- Do they seek counsel?
- Tie up any loose ends, i.e. exes
- Show growth, self-discovery, new strength and resolve
- Do not pull magic out of a hat, or misunderstanding resolved by a random remark or circumstance. H/h must EARN their HEA by dealing with their issues.

Grand Romantic Moment – The Climax

- This is the final confrontation. The one who did the most hurting, running, or had the most doubts usually initiates
- Show true change and inner conflicts resolved. Make it believable.

- All armor is removed, they bare their souls, show their true selves
- Enemies and opposition are defeated, and Love is declared and accepted!

Resolution or Epilogue

- Complete the circle!
- Show Hero and Heroine in changed state with family, friends, etc.
- Wrap up any other tiny loose ends
- Love scene optional, but should leave reader with a warm and satisfied feeling.
- Closing scene completes theme. What is the takeaway message?

Novella Writing Schedule

- Decide on a target word count, 20K, 30K, 40K, 48K
- Divide Word Count into 8 pieces.
- Use these 1/8 markers to pace yourself. You don't have to be exact, but it helps to reel you in if you know you have to hit the next marker.
- Example: 40K/8 = 5000 words
- Don't sweat it if you're not exact!

Novella Markers (Part 1)

- 1/8: 0-5K – Hook and Inciting Incident, First Meet, cute or otherwise
- 2/8: 5-10K – Lock-In/Core Conflict
- 3/8: 10-15K – Fun and Games, Raise Emotional Stakes, Introduce Opposition, Start Subplot
- 4/8: 15-20K – I'm in Love, Midpoint Reversal, this affair is serious and life-changing.

Novella Markers (Part 2)

- 5/8: 20-25K – Magnify Conflict, Show how GOOD love is
- 6/8: 25K-30K – Dark Moment, Remaining flaws and wounds cause all hope to be lost.
- 7/8: 30K-35K – Recovery, Seek Counsel, Make Changes, End Subplot
- 8/8: 35K-40K – Climax and Resolution, Grand Romantic Moment and HEA, Thematic Closure

Perfect Novella Tropes

- Second Chance – characters have a history. Don't need to show initial attraction and ramp up.
- Crush from the Past – one character already is attracted to other. Can bring in family, schoolmates, knowledge of past to pursue the other.
- Vacation/Holiday Affair – Limited time period. Away from normal life. Feeling of carelessness and going for it.

Difficult Novella Tropes

- Opposites Attract, Enemies to Lovers, Forbidden Lover – must overcome the reason they are opposites or enemies or forbidden. High level of conflict.
- Friends to Lovers, Best Friend or Sibling's Ex – takes subplots to expose why they should change existing relationship, family issues and drama.
- Fake It, pretend relationship. Need to overcome the pretense and realize this is real. Family or others are involved, lies and secrets need resolution

Neutral Novella Tropes

- Instant Love, Love at First Sight – quickly gets to love scenes, must explain continued attraction
- Single Parent – good if child is an ally, not good if child is opposition.
- One Night Stand, usually involves a Bet or a Dare. Or Rebound. Both parties motivated to initiate romance. Need reason to sustain.

Pitfalls of Romance Novella

- Insta-Love, inadequate preparation
- Predictable Conflicts, clichéd plot
- Whiplash [loves me, loves me not]
- Jumping Conflict, one issue not resolved before going to the next
- Rushed Love Scenes, wham-bam
- Missing Emotional Depth
- Sudden, unexplained turnaround
- Too easy, quick HEA, fairy godmother

Questions?

- Did you enjoy writing a novella?

- Did you feel it was different from writing a full-length novel? In what way, good or bad?
- Did my timeline/schedule help you even if you are a pantser? Did you use it?
- Did you find the slides and exercise helpful? Any other questions or comments? THANKS for participating!

Publishing Your Novella

If you are self-publishing your novella, you would follow the same method as you do in publishing a full length work. Editing, proofreading, preparing a book cover, and formatting all needs to be done.

Since many editors charge by the page or word count, you will likely pay less for these services.

Because you are now writing more stories at a faster pace, your cost for cover art is likely to go up unless you learn to make your own covers.

The same could be said for ebook and print book formatting. Again, if you learn how to do it yourself, you will come out ahead.

The other question is what to charge for your novella. You will likely charge less than for your full-length novels, but the real opportunity lies in boxing up your novellas into a boxed set and offering a slight discount over single copy prices.

Readers love boxed sets because they view it as a value buy.

You can publish your novella in either multi- or single author boxed sets, and you can also choose to make a novella free as a gift to readers in your mailing list, or as an incentive to sign up for your list.

There is also a renewed interest by traditional publishers in bundling theme-based novellas, especially around the holidays. Many publishers have ebook-only lines that make publishing novellas, shorter works, and bundles more financially viable.

You can also look for small presses, some which are electronic only, who run their own e-stores, or submit your novella to contests, periodicals, and literary journals. While it's not impossible to get a large traditional publisher to pick up your novella, it works better if it is part of a larger series, maybe as a prequel or a holiday special for something already established.

The possibilities are endless, and I hope you agree with me that a well written novella is a wonderful vehicle in increasing your author presence, sales, and readership.

Pitfalls of Writing a Novella

Now that I have you interested in writing a novella, I must warn you of some common pitfalls. I went through Amazon and read reviews. I also downloaded and read many novellas, mostly in the romance genre.

Here are some common problems with the execution of a novella.

Not making the case

Loose ends

Problem not solved

Cardboard characters

Ending comes from nowhere

Too predictable

Inadequate character motivation

Can't feel the relationship

Unsatisfactory character development

Missing emotional depth

Storyline is condensed, more telling than showing

No story arc, randomly following characters around and then the story is cut.

Unnecessary cliffhangers. This follows from not having a story arc.

Missing backstory, background

Less descriptive, could not get a feel for the surroundings and the setting where the characters are coming from

Abbreviated, no great depth

Reads like a plot outline

Puppet-like characters doing things because it's time to do them, not because it follows naturally.

Not worth the money.

No time to relax, no time to immerse in the story world

Watching strangers do and say things

Choppy, end came too quickly

Last Word

While we concentrated on the benefits of writing a novella, don't neglect your full-length novels. Readers who are hooked on your writing style will tell you they prefer longer works. They love your voice and your characters and want to spend more time with them.

Also, never shortchange your story. If your characters need the time, go long. Don't cut things off because you are determined to write a novella. Don't make the mistake of introducing deep conflicts with high levels of drama and emotional overtones and then cutting it short—summarizing things at the end and leaving the reader hanging.

Your job is to take the reader on an emotional journey, not leave them stranded right when things are getting good. The story has to go where it wants to go and be complete. It has to be as rich as it needs to be and as involved as it has to be. Don't make the mistake of confusing a novella with a barebones outline form. A novella is fundamentally suited to an easily solved story problem, a light romp in the park, and a delightful snack. Think of it this way, if you cram a five course meal into the space a coffee break and give your guests one teaspoon for every course, how satisfied would they be? Here, have a cube of steak, a teaspoon of soup, one arugula leaf and a candied walnut piece, and a thimble full of chocolate mousse for dessert.

I've seen this done (not the dinner party) and believe me, it's unsatisfying. Because of the need to cram or a rush to finish, the author ends up doing a lot of telling to wrap up the story.

So, when you're writing, and you have the urge to finish with a quick summary list to wrap things up, ask yourself why? Did you open up too many doors and now you have to close them? If you opened too many doors, were all of them necessary to the story? If not, go back and cut them.

If the open questions were necessary and key to the story, then take your time in resolving them. If your word count goes higher, so be it.

Remember, the last impression you leave is the one your reader will carry. So, while you want to leave your readers wanting a little more, make sure they're not wanting too much more.

Thank you for reading through my guide on writing a romance novella. While writing speed varies, I do believe that if you follow my schedule and do the exercises, that you will be able to finish your romance novella in thirty days or less.

Please drop me a line at ayala.rachelle@gmail.com if you have any comments or would like to join my Romance In A Month Facebook group.

Best of all luck on your writing, and please consider writing a review if this book has been helpful to you.

Thanks and Happy Writing!

About the Author

Rachelle Ayala is a bestselling author of dramatic romantic suspense and humorous, sexy contemporary romances. Her heroines are feisty and her heroes hot. She writes emotionally challenging stories but believes in the power of love and hope.

Rachelle is the founder of an online writing group, Romance in a Month, an active member of the California Writer's Club, Fremont Chapter, and a volunteer for the World Literary Cafe. She has won the 2015 Angie Ovation Award for *Knowing Vera* as well as the 2015 Readers' Favorite Gold Award for *A Father for Christmas*.

Check out her Reader's Guide at
http://rachelleayala.net/books

NOTES

NOTES

NOTES

NOTES

Printed in Great Britain
by Amazon

81427016R00068